LCM:

The Secret to Success in the New Age of Real Estate

LCM:

The Secret to Success in the New Age of Real Estate

Matt Jones

Published by:
Favorite Agent Publishing
4155 Ferncreek Drive
Fayetteville, NC 28314
www.lcmbook.com

Copyright © 2005 Matt Jones
Interior text design by Tom Davis
ISBN: 0-9770438-0-0
Library of Congress Control Number: 2005930523

LCM: The Secret to Success in the New Age of Real Estate.
All rights reserved. Except for brief excerpts used in reviews, no portion of this work may be reproduced or published without expressed written permission from the author or the author's agent.

First Edition
Printed and bound in the United States of America by Morris Publishing • www.morrispublishing.com • 800-650-7888
1 2 3 4 5 6 7 8 9 10

ACKNOWLEDGEMENT

As I sit down to write this acknowledgement, it's hard to know where to begin. The fact is that I've been very blessed in my short real estate career, and I want to give credit where credit is due. But I'd be remiss if I didn't start by thanking God for His inspiration, guidance, and blessing along the way, without which none of my success would have been either possible or enjoyable.

I'm also very grateful to my fellow real estate professionals here in Fayetteville, North Carolina, who have sold listings, challenged me to greatness, and in general been very helpful to me while I've been learning this new and phenomenal business. There are so many of you who have shaped my success that it's impossible to name all of you. It's an honor to be associated with such a group.

Next I want to say that, when I knew next to nothing about real estate, when all it meant to me was a house that wouldn't sell or another sign up in the neighborhood, there was my good friend, my very first broker and real estate mentor, David Evans, who somehow managed to talk me right into the business.

Finally, I want to mention Zan Monroe, executive director of the Fayetteville Association of Realtors, whose thoughtful, levelheaded advice has never failed me. Whenever I insisted on thinking too far outside the box, he was there to keep me from getting myself in trouble.

My sincere thanks to all of you. Your influence is everywhere in the pages of this book.

CONTENTS

Introduction 9

Chapter 1 - Foundations 17
    The State of Our Industry 18
    Who Am I, and What Gives Me the Right to Speak? .. 21
    How to Get the Most from Reading This Book 22

Chapter 2 - My Listing Presentation: Doing the Prep Work   25
    Ethics and Listing at 8% Commission 25
    Becoming the Market Authority 27
    The Credibility Factor 34
    Summing It Up 35

Chapter 3 - My Listing Presentation:
    How and Why It Works 37
    The Ultimate CMA 38
    Putting the Pieces Together 41
    Two Ways to Sell the House 42

Chapter 4 - My Listing Presentation:
    What to Say and How to Say It 49
    What to Say and How to Say it 50
    Taking Listings over the Phone 54
    Real-life Examples 59

Chapter 5 - Getting Business to Come to You 65
    The Secret of My Success 66
    Getting Business to Come to You 76

Chapter 6 – How to Tap the Internet Effectively 81
   Today's Agents Must Tap the Web 82
   An Internet Advertising Primer 83
   Internet Real Estate for Dummies 86
   Using Technology to Gain Share in a Crowded Market 92
   I'm Just Looking! 93

Chapter 7 – Taking Your Business to the Next Level:
   Becoming a Rainmaker 99
   How to Build a Team 100
   When to Move to Management 104
   Closing Thoughts 108

Afterword 111

About the Author 113

INTRODUCTION

Dear Fellow REALTOR®,

Thank you for your interest in LCM. I'm excited to have this opportunity to share my book with you! It's my sincere hope that it will be inspirational to you—that it will be instrumental in transforming your real estate practice. Whether you're a new agent struggling to get started or a seasoned professional looking for a breakthrough to the next level of success, I truly believe that you'll find realistic, practical help and encouragement in *LCM*.

I will be quick to tell you that I really don't like reading books filled with "fluff," and I promise that *this* will not be one. This book could easily have been twice as long, but – and I'm sure you'll appreciate this — I don't want to waste your time with filler just for the sake of adding length. But the book's brevity also means that I'm not going to say the same thing again and again just to make a point. If you don't read what I've written carefully, you may miss a lot. I will make you one promise at the outset, though: if you'll read *LCM* carefully and then put into practice the things I've taught you, that information will make you a lot of money.

However, before you jump in, thinking that this is a get-rich-quick scheme, I want to assure you that nothing could be further from the truth. *There is no surefire way to wealth without hard work.* BUT the process will be much easier if you work smart *and* hard. In this book, I will show you some ways to do exactly that and, in the process, take your business to a level you never thought you'd reach. My hope is that you'll approach this book as seriously as you would a very important college course. There's homework (but not much), and there's some content that will be difficult; but by the time you finish the book, I believe you'll have the basic framework on which to build a very successful real estate practice. Make no mistake, though: it'll all be up to you. So how badly do you want to get to the next level?

When I started in real estate, I had a plan (and that was a good thing!), but much of my plan was based on flawed or bad information. I assumed that a majority of what I had read in real estate how-to books and listened to on tapes and in classes would work for me. Was I in for a rude awakening! Although much of what I had been taught about how to succeed in real estate (farming, circle-of-influence marketing, direct mail, cold calling, walking the neighborhoods, sitting open houses, and many other strategies) provided some measure of success, it simply didn't generate the level of income I'd entered the profession to earn.

In fact, after about three months on the job I was at the point of throwing in the towel. I was accustomed to earning a six-figure income, but with my new real estate career I was on my way to making only about $30,000 (approximately what the average REALTOR® in the US makes per year). It occurred to me that, if I wanted to do like all the other agents, I would always earn what all the other agents earned. And guess what? That was simply not acceptable to me. Is it to you? I hope not!

So after coming to this realization, I pretty much set aside all that the experts had taught me about marketing and real estate. Calling up my previous business and technology experience, I started over from scratch. My goal was to be as different as possible from the other agents, and I soon realized that my instincts were excellent. Amazing things began to happen almost overnight! Instead of being a very frustrated and unfulfilled REALTOR®, suddenly I was a top producer. Within another three months, my practice had grown so fast that I hired my first buyer's agent. Then another. Then another. Before long, I was spending as much time recruiting agents to help me as I was selling real estate.

Now it's been almost three years, and business has never slowed down. Never! And I'm here to tell you that this same kind of thing can happen for you. If you have the guts to abandon what's not working (or maybe working only marginally) and start doing what *will* work, you can have the same kind of result. Maybe even better!

Part of my job as a REALTOR® and broker is managing agents and creating a friendly and productive work environment. As I write this page, I can't help thinking about how far I've come in such a short time. When I entered the real estate business, I completed one transaction in three months. This year I will average three transactions per *day*! My solo practice has evolved into a company of 38 agents. And what used to be the 386th largest company in our community is now fourth. Better still, we succeeded so quickly! This year we should do approximately 900 transactions and grow to about 75 agents.

So how did we progress so quickly? Well, actually, the answer is in this book.

I have a very simple philosophy: if I make those agents around me successful, I will succeed. The scripture says, "Whatsoever a man soweth, that shall he also reap." Therefore, if I wish to reap the *benefits* of success, I must sow the *seeds* of success. That's what I try to do, and the results are astounding. We have one of the happiest companies I've ever seen. No fussing or feuding. No bickering among agents. No office politics. We have an unbelievably pleasant work environment because we don't have the main problem causing strife and discontent in real estate brokerages today: we don't have *lead scarcity*. In addition, hardly a day goes by that we aren't approached by a local REALTOR® asking to join our company. Obviously, that's not how it is in most businesses. (Maybe you know first-hand.) This year, more than 350,000 agents will leave our industry because they haven't been able to succeed financially. What a shame!

If ever there was a time to be in real estate, that time is now! But whatever worked years ago simply isn't working any more. Many long-term agents have built such a book of business that they're still able to make a good living; but if they're really honest, they will generally tell you that they're working harder than ever for the same amount of money. Yet the problem isn't the agents: it's their "old school" methods. Why? First, our culture is changing rapidly, and traditional real estate is very culture-based. Even more importantly, technology has drastically influenced the way people go about buying and selling homes – yet most agents are still using the old methods and tools on their new customers, often to their own peril. So again I say, what a shame! Things don't have to be done that way! In this book I promise to open your eyes to some new strategies that will transform forever the way you do real estate. But in order for these strategies to work for you, you will have to read them, study them, and put them into practice.

LCM, the title of this book, could easily stand for *Listings, Customers, and Money* (although it doesn't). But, in fact, here is a formula that you can write down:

$$\text{Listings} + \text{Customers} = \text{Money}$$

Now let's look at it again. If you want to make money, you need to have two things: listings and customers. Each will get you the other. If you have listings, you will get calls from home buyers looking for homes and from home owners needing help selling. I know that many of you reading this book right now are either listing agents or buyers' agents exclusively, and that's okay.

There are strategies and techniques for listing agents. In fact, the first few chapters of this book cover only my listing presentation, and I promise that you've never seen anything quite like it. What we're doing could not be farther from the same old thing! And if you're a buyer's agent, I promise that there will be a lot of good stuff in this book for you too. I simply had to start somewhere. And since I believe that listing is the most important step in the real estate process, I started there.

Now, whether you're a buyer agent or a listing agent, the *lead scarcity* that I mentioned earlier is your biggest headache. To put it another way, the problem in most real estate companies is that there isn't enough business to go around. So even though most agents are reasonably pleasant people, when they have to worry about supporting their families, they feel anxiety, and that anxiety translates into workplace unrest.

If you've been an agent for several years, think about it: getting new business used to be much easier than it is today. With lead generation companies springing up every day now, many potential customers are being siphoned out of the market before we even have a chance to talk with them. Then, to add insult to injury, those same aggregators have the nerve to "sell" our customers back to us as leads!

Well, I'm happy to say that things don't have to be that way. You don't have to be at the mercy of the lead aggregators. You can generate your *own* customers—more than you can ever handle!—if you apply to your job what you learn in this book. Wouldn't it be nice to have more business than you could do? Wouldn't it be great to have the luxury of being able to refer that occasional "problem" customer to another agent? Well, it can happen. In these chapters, you will find the secret to solving the "lead scarcity" problem. You'll learn how to create a huge base of business—so big that you may decide to grow your own team or even your own company. Maybe you'll even refer the additional business to other agents for a fee!

I hope that I've given you enough of a reason to read this book. Again, I pledge that if you invest your time in reading the book and then applying the lessons you've learned from it to the development of your own business, your real estate life will never again be the same. This is my sincere promise.

It will be my great honor to be able to play a part in your future success.

CHAPTER 1 — FOUNDATIONS

INSIDE CHAPTER ONE

- THE STATE OF THE INDUSTRY
- WHO AM I, AND WHAT GIVES ME THE RIGHT TO SPEAK?
- WHAT TO EXPECT IN THIS BOOK
- HOW TO GET THE MOST FROM READING THIS BOOK

As I sat down to write this chapter, I was interrupted—not by one of those bad interruptions, but a good one. As our company grows, one of the tasks that I've kept on *my* list is the writing of agent commission checks. It keeps me plugged into our local real estate team and gives me a feel for who's doing what. Anyway, I interrupted the book writing to sign five agent commission checks, one of which was for $7200 to one of our newer agents!

But here's the really cool part: Joe (the new agent) had listed this home at 8% (within a week after taking our listing training) and sold it the same day he listed it by using our approach. He was so excited he could hardly contain himself! The truth, though, is that any agent can benefit from this approach to listing if he takes the time to learn it and apply the principles that I will share here. We teach it to all of our agents, and we have agent partners using it all across the US and Canada, with the same or similar results.

I've mentioned that happy experience so that I can now say this: *LCM* is one of the most important books you may ever read on the subject of real estate. If you allow yourself to absorb the information and the techniques that I'm going to share, they can truly revolutionize the way you practice real estate and dramatically change your income level for the better. What's even more important is that this book will actually improve your service to your clients!

THE STATE OF OUR INDUSTRY

Today there are more new homes being built than ever before. Home prices are at an all-time high, whereas interest rates have reached almost unprecedented lows, giving today's home buyers more purchasing power than at any time in the past four decades. Technology has shortened the home-search process by a third. There are more mortgage products on the market than ever before, allowing more people than ever to qualify for loans. Our economy is robust and in the midst of a major recovery. And a whole new generation of home buyers are entering the market as first-time homeowners. What a day to be in real estate!

Does this sound like good news? It's GREAT news! Yet, in spite of all the optimism and all the success stories, a third of all REALTORS® will fail in business this year. A third! Most will leave the industry, even though this is undoubtedly one of the best times ever to be in real estate.

But guess what? Regardless of what you may have been told at the latest "scare-'em-to-death" seminars, the discount firms are *not* making substantial inroads, even in the most competitive markets. The banks are *not* taking over the world of real estate. Many large companies have been working on national FSBO web sites and national MLS web sites, all with public access; yet even though they may shape our industry, the big guys will *not*, in my opinion, destroy it. The fact is that individual homeowners want to work with professionals. Now, what a professional may look like in ten years may surprise us all. But the fact is that *we have job security*.

The reason that REALTORS® are leaving our industry in droves is that they can't make a decent living. And the reason they can't make a decent living is that most of them cannot figure out how to get enough business. For one thing, our real estate schooling teaches them what *not* to do, and then the firm that hires them has to turn around and teach them what *to* do. Many brokers don't have a clue about what's going on in our vastly changing industry. They're as lost as the new agents they're hiring!

The standard techniques and strategies that worked a decade ago are *no longer working*. So what do I mean? Farming. Circle-of-influence (sphere-of-influence) marketing. Walking neighborhoods. Calling on FSBOs. Calling on expireds. Sitting open houses. Floor duty. Desk time. Networking. Direct mail. Cold calling. (In fact, if you're not careful with your cold calling, you could land yourself a huge fine!) All of these historically proven and accepted methods of lead generation are barely working today. As I speak to agents across the country, they tell me they're struggling like never before. Even veterans of twenty-plus years are finding that the job is getting harder, when it should be doing just the opposite. It's not your imagination if you think it's getting tougher out there. For too many agents, it *is*!

And yet...top producers are making more money than ever before. It's not uncommon to see real estate agents earning seven figures – some after only a few years in the business. In fact, I'll earn seven figures this year from my real estate company alone, and I'm still the new kid in the industry! There's no reason that anyone willing to work hard and work smart can't experience the same level of success.

WHO AM I, AND WHAT GIVES ME THE RIGHT TO SPEAK?

So you may be asking yourself, "What makes *him* an authority all of a sudden?" After all, I'm a relatively new real estate agent, and there are countless REALTORS® with more experience than me. Then too, I didn't grow up in a real estate family or spend a lot of time in formal real estate training. I don't have many certifications or initials after my name, and I'm not in a "super" real estate market.

What I am is just an average person with a lot of determination and will to succeed. It's also true that I practice real estate in a below-average market, but I came into the industry from a technology background that gave me a unique perspective. And the timing was right: the real estate industry was undergoing a fundamental change, and I had exactly the right background for it, at exactly the right moment. Because I didn't have extensive previous experience, I had no problem looking outside the box. In fact, I didn't even know there *was* a box!

During my first twelve months in real estate, I listed 74 properties, and no, I didn't have a builder listing. These were individual homeowners wanting to sell their homes. In my first calendar year I listed 114 individual homes. And although I'm in a market that typically lists for 6% or less, I listed every home at 8% or more! Some were as high as 12%!

As I write this, I've been in real estate for less than three years. In that short time, as I mentioned in the Introduction, I've grown from a single-agent practice to a full-blown, 38-member brokerage that constantly adds agents and staff. Since becoming our own brokerage nine months ago, we've gone from last place to fourth in our market. And if we continue at our current rate, we'll be the largest company in this market in less than twenty-four months! We expect to do over $113 million in production this year.

Since April 2004, agent partners in more than 500 markets across the US and Canada have begun using the technology that we developed, and every single day we receive applications from thirty to fifty potential agent partners wanting to use our technology to accomplish the same things in their own markets. In addition, many of them are already beginning to see some of the same level of success.

HOW TO GET THE MOST FROM READING THIS BOOK

You will take away from this book exactly what you put into it. If you don't exert the effort to study the information, it will probably have very little impact on your business. On the other hand, if you focus on the ideas and concepts in *LCM* and then take the steps to implement them into your own practice, this simple book could truly make you hundreds of thousands of dollars. No kidding!

The next chapter will introduce you to my listing presentation, and you will not want to miss it! I can assure you that you haven't heard anything even remotely similar to it, and you'll be amazed at how simple, yet effective, it is. In a time when our industry is trending downward in commissions, you can actually increase your commissions without putting your clients at a disadvantage.

CHAPTER 2—
MY LISTING PRESENTATION: DOING THE PREP WORK

INSIDE CHAPTER TWO:

- ETHICS AND LISTING AT 8% COMMISSION
- BECOMING THE MARKET AUTHORITY
- THE CREDIBILITY FACTOR
- SUMMING IT UP

This listing presentation will show you how to list at 8% commission *virtually every single time*! Oh, I know that statement sounds incredible, but it's true! There's no reason that you can't list for 8% or even more. The secret is in this presentation.

ETHICS AND LISTING AT 8% COMMISSION

Okay, before we dive into the presentation, it's important that we first mention ethics. In other words, "How can I better serve my clients while charging them more?"

Simply by having that thought, you've confirmed that you're an ethical REALTOR® who's trying to put your clients' interests first. That's a good thing. Having said it, though, I need to underscore the fallacy in such a line of thinking. The question we've asked seems to imply that you *cannot* earn good money by doing the right thing. But the truth is that it's possible to serve your clients, your fellow REALTORS®, and yourself; and with this presentation it's also easy! Let me explain.

We'll begin by discussing agency—specifically, seller agency. As a listing agent, your client is the seller in any transaction. You're the seller's agent, though, and you have a fiduciary obligation to represent him or her to the best of your ability. As a rule, you should be trying to get your client the most money in the shortest amount of time, since that's the goal with most sellers. And when I mention "money," I specifically mean *net* dollars. Ultimately it doesn't matter how large or small the commission is: what counts is the total taken away from the closing table.

So if you knew about a strategy that would net your client more money while selling his home in only about half the usual time, wouldn't it be in his interest to use it? Of course it would! Well, that's what this listing presentation will do for you. As compared with traditional listings of homes in the same market, my presentation will give you a strategy that has traditionally netted my clients 2.7% more money while selling their homes in only 55% of the average DOM (number of days on market).

More money in half the time! Think of it! Your clients (and the other agents in the market) will love you, you'll be paid better in the process, and you'll begin to acquire a reputation for being the agent with the high-paying listings.

But I'm getting ahead of myself. Let's take this thing one step at a time.

So...on the flip side, if you knew that selling a house by the traditional method would double your client's waiting time and, in the process, net him *less money*, would that be good for him? Of course not! Not even if you saved him some money in commissions! Your job as a listing agent is to represent the seller and to place his needs *first*, and that's what we're going to do.

BECOMING THE MARKET AUTHORITY

Before we get into the listing presentation, it's important for you to do an honest assessment of your ability as an agent. Can you look into the mirror and feel, deep down, that you are the very best person to represent your seller client? If you can't do that (regardless of the listing approach you use), it would be unethical to offer your services to this client in the first place. In fact, you'd have a fiduciary obligation to recommend your fellow agent, Mr. or Ms. So-and-So, as the best agent to help him.

So how do you go about creating in yourself the best agent to represent your client? You need to do your homework! You need to study your market. You need to know the market statistics. You need to have clear-cut marketing strategies. You need to have a specific marketing plan that will yield results *superior* to those of the competition. Otherwise, you have nothing to offer the client! Doesn't that make sense? Why should your client list his most valuable asset with you if you don't know what you're doing? Would *you* list with yourself? And if your answer to my last question isn't a resounding "Yes!" — then you need to become that ideal agent before you read another word in this book.

Prior to listing the first house, I knew our market statistics cold. I pulled the raw data from our local MLS and crunched the numbers. Was it fun? Of course not! Nevertheless, *I needed to know what I was talking about.*

Trust me about this: your client will recognize whether or not you know what you're talking about. If you're bluffing, he'll sense it. You can't "fake the funk," as they say. I can't tell you how many times a listing client has quoted an agent on something that I've known to be incorrect. Because I was completely familiar with my market, though, I would be able to explain that the agent, while very likely a nice person, had his facts wrong. Then I would lay the statistics on the client, and it was quite obvious to both of us that I knew what I was doing.

Here's the basic market data you need to know before you go to your first listing appointment:

1) <u>Days on Market (DOM)</u>. Average days on market is critical to your seller client for several reasons: it's important in setting realistic expectations about the time needed to sell a home; it will help you evaluate any offers that come in and make an educated decision about whether it's advisable for the client to wait for another offer or take what's on the table; and, if you know the DOM for your market (or, better, yet, for the client's neighborhood), you'll be able to guide him or her through the process like a professional – which is exactly what you are!

There's a problem with DOM statistics, however. Most MLS databases have a much-manipulated DOM number which is invariably skewed low. So how can you know what the real number is? Is it possible to determine the actual DOM for your market even if you're not a rocket scientist? Absolutely! Just use the absorption rate to calculate the true DOM for your area. Let me explain.

Here's how you get the real DOM. Find out how many homes sold in your market last year *and* how many are *currently* on the market. For example, if 10,000 homes sold last year, and there are currently 5000 on the market, what those numbers indicate is that the inventory turned twice last year (10,000/5000 = 2.0). Now, there are twelve months in a year, and 12/2.0 = 6.0, which is the absorption rate, meaning that the average time *actually* on market is 6.0 months. So to convert the absorption rate to days on market, you simply multiply this last number by 30 (6.0 x 30 = 180). And if you figure DOM this way, you'll eliminate all manipulation in your market by builders and agents who re-list stigmatized homes, which of course are those homes that have picked up a negative image due to their excessive time on market.

2) <u>DOM Standard Deviation (STDEV)</u>. What?! By now you're thinking, "Matt Jones has lost his mind!" Before you dismiss this concept (and me) as crazy, though, let me point out that it will be an easy statistic to calculate and a powerful advantage for you once you know it.

So how do you calculate it? The easiest way to calculate DOM STDEV is by using a spreadsheet such as Microsoft Excel. On your computer, pull up all the closed residential properties for your community from the last year. You'll want to pull them up in your MLS, using a one-liner format. Then copy and paste that data onto a spreadsheet.

Next you'll want to delete all but three of the columns: list price, sale price, and DOM. At the bottom of each of these columns, calculate the average and the standard deviation. If you're using Excel, the function will look like this: =average(b1:b20000) and =stdev(b1:b20000). Both of these examples assume that you're calculating the average and the standard deviation for column B and that there are numbers in the rows from 1 through 20,000.

Okay, you have the numbers, so let's assume that the standard deviation of the DOM is 53 days. If so, your absorption method will indicate that the true DOM is 186 days. Now comes the fun part! Add one standard deviation (53 days) to your average of 186, and you have 239 days. Add another standard deviation, and you have 292 days. Here's what that means for your listing client:

> You have a 50% chance of selling his home in the average DOM. If you add one standard deviation, you take the probabilities to 84%, and if you add another standard deviation, it's 93%. Another standard deviation would elevate the probabilities to 96%, then to 98%, and so on. Now let's say that a competing REALTOR® tries to convince your client that his home can sell in

a matter of days and that he should list for ninety days.

You can tell your client with complete certainty that the statistical probability of selling his home in a few days is nil, and that in reality he should expect the process to take the average amount of time plus at least one standard deviation. Using the illustration above, you should inform him that he has a 93% probability of selling his home in 292 days, using the typical approach. If that's how long, statistically, it'll take to sell his house, then listing it for ninety days will clearly be a waste of everyone's time.

Now, your immediate reaction may be that your clients will never go for this system — yet they will! In all but one of my listings I received one-year terms, and in the remaining listing I got a six-month term, knowing that I would sell the house even sooner. When you tell a client, with authority, how long it will take to sell his home, he'll inevitably respect your honesty and the fact that you know exactly what it takes to sell a home in your market. You're not guessing, like most agents, and in fact you're speaking with the voice of authority. Knowing your market better than any other agent will impress your clients while also giving your own confidence level a boost.

3) <u>Average Markdown (List/Sale Ratio)</u>. Now let's go back to the statistics that we worked on earlier. Remember my asking you to calculate the average for list price and sale price? Here's the reason: you need to be able to advise your client as to the "typical" discount in your market. Let's assume that the average listing price is $175,000, and the average sale price is $169,000. Now, subtract the average sale price from the average listing price, and then divide the difference by the average listing price.

$175,000 - $169,000 = $6000
$6000/$175,000 = 0.034, or 3.4% markdown

In other words, your client should understand that it's normal in your market to expect a markdown (or discount) of 3.4% from the listing price. Setting expectations shows him that you understand the market and that you'll help prepare him for the offers that will be coming in. You'll also have an advantage in negotiating with other agents when you know that the average markdown in a certain neighborhood is only 0.5%, while *they're* offering 4% below the asking price! You can tell an agent that it's unreasonable to expect your client to accept such a figure and that he should encourage *his* client to make a more reasonable offer. I can't tell you how many times this simple formula has made thousands of dollars for my clients because I knew the market statistics, and the other agents didn't.

THE CREDIBILITY FACTOR

Let me leave you with one example of how this statistical knowledge can influence your credibility. Imagine a client with a nice home worth roughly $500,000, and now imagine *you* going up against the top listing agent in your market. How do you feel? Are you nervous? This guy has lots of signs all over the area. Who are you? Just some new agent without many listings?

Now imagine that the top dog is a typical agent who doesn't know anything, really, about the local market. He'll talk in generalities about how good he is at selling homes and how quickly he expects to sell this one.

But because you know the market data, you go into the listing presentation *ready*. You tell the seller that homes in his price tier have a DOM of 289 and that, with the standard deviation of 72, he has an 84% chance of selling the home within 361 days (basically a year). Furthermore, in order to have 9:1 odds of selling the home, he'll need to wait 433 days if he uses the traditional approach. The agent promising to sell the house in only a few days is being dishonest or, at the least, confused (or overly optimistic!) because the probability of selling the home in fewer than 145 days is under 7%.

Then you begin to show this potential client a better way, a way that will more than double the chances of selling his home *while netting him more money*. Guess what? You've just landed a really nice listing. And why? Because you're the best agent to sell it! And now that you're the best, you can sell the listing with authority. You're the best, you know it, and now the client knows it too. Most importantly, you've got the listing!

SUMMING IT UP

I think you'll agree that this is a lot of information to digest! So I suggest that you look through it a few more times until it makes perfect sense. It's important that you master the basics before we build on them with the listing presentation. Why? Because the presentation requires that you be utterly confident in whatever approach you use. You need to become the best agent you can be. You owe this much to your clients, and you owe it to yourself.

To summarize: we've learned that it's ethical to list at 8% (assuming that the listing will net your client more money and sell his home in less time); but we've also learned that it's *un*ethical *not* to use this approach if you know it'll deliver better results (which it will). Your seller client is entitled to the best representation he can get. Let it be you!

So how do you start off down the path toward becoming a great listing agent? First, be the best agent for the job. You have to know your market numbers cold.

Statistics can be mind-numbing, but the few simple statistics we've mentioned are absolutely worth learning. Imagine a bell curve. The centerline of this curve is the average, or 50% probability. If you move to the right or left of the centerline by one standard deviation, you cover the odds from 16% on the low end of the center to 84% on the high end. A second standard deviation reveals a 7%-to-93% probability. The average markdown will assist you in building expectations for your client and for the other agents, and the process is much easier than it appears. In fact, it's far easier than reading a HUD-1 or calculating interim interest!

In the next part of the listing presentation, we'll discuss how to take this knowledge base and convert it into premium listings. You'll be amazed when clients actually ask you to list their homes at 8% or even more! Not only can it happen; it *will* happen when you use this approach to selling houses. Do your homework! Learn your market numbers. In only a few hours you'll have them nailed down.

So now you've taken the first step toward becoming the dominant listing agent in your market!

CHAPTER 3 —
MY LISTING PRESENTATION: HOW AND WHY IT WORKS

INSIDE CHAPTER THREE:

- THE ULTIMATE CMA
- PUTTING THE PIECES TOGETHER
- TWO WAYS TO SELL THE HOUSE

In the previous chapter we talked about your becoming the best agent for the job. We mentioned the importance of learning your market statistics and told you exactly how to do that. We discussed how you could increase your credibility and power by arming yourself with some very specific knowledge. I'll assume that you've done your homework now and are ready to learn the actual listing presentation that made me one of the top listing agents in the country.

I want you to notice that I haven't referred to myself as one of the *smartest* agents in the country because there are plenty of agents who are smarter than me. I haven't claimed that I'm the *hardest-working* agent in the country because there are lots of hard-working agents. But I do maintain that I'm one of the top listing agents because there are very, very few agents who have listed as many homes in a single year as I have, and even fewer who have listed all of their homes for 8% or more. *And* there are fewer yet who have netted their clients 2.7% *more money at closing* while selling their homes *twice as fast* as most of the agents in their markets.

So how do I do it? I use a unique system that I call "the traffic approach." In a few minutes we'll get into this approach to listing, but first we need to examine how I go about doing a CMA (comparative market analysis).

THE ULTIMATE CMA

Anyone who knows numbers can tell you that, as a listing agent using the traditional method of doing a CMA, you can make the numbers say anything you want. Here's what I mean.

> With the traditional CMA method, the agent selects three recently-sold properties that closely represent the subject home (or the home being valued). In most markets, it's easy to find three properties that sold high, three that sold average, and three that sold low and still have many other comps from which to choose.

What many agents do (and what they teach) is to use the least expensive set of comps for the CMA. This method makes the case for listing the home as inexpensively as possible and allows it to sell quickly. However, as a seller's agent you should be getting your client the most money for his property, not co-conspiring in a giveaway.

What *I* do in preparing a CMA is to take data from three sources: tax records (sale and assessment data), the closed comparable listings in the MLS, and the active comparable listings in the MLS. Let me explain.

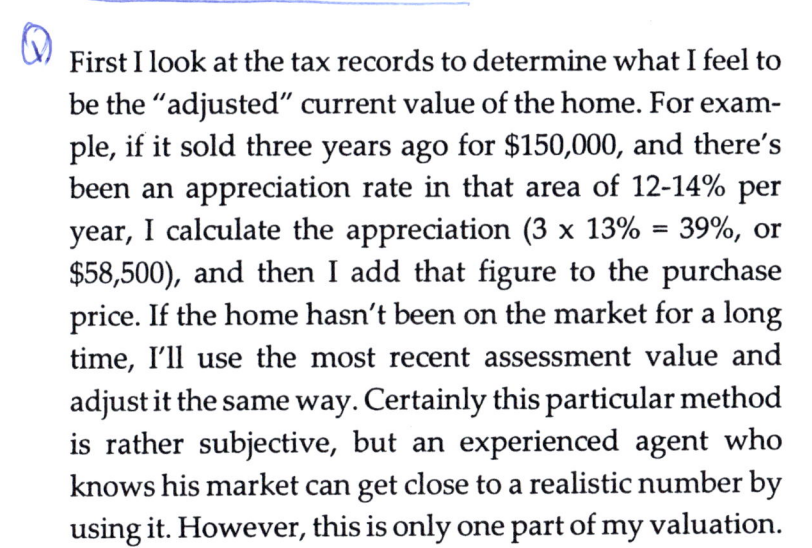

First I look at the tax records to determine what I feel to be the "adjusted" current value of the home. For example, if it sold three years ago for $150,000, and there's been an appreciation rate in that area of 12-14% per year, I calculate the appreciation (3 x 13% = 39%, or $58,500), and then I add that figure to the purchase price. If the home hasn't been on the market for a long time, I'll use the most recent assessment value and adjust it the same way. Certainly this particular method is rather subjective, but an experienced agent who knows his market can get close to a realistic number by using it. However, this is only one part of my valuation.

Next I pull up all the closed comparables in the area or subdivision, going back a reasonable period of time, and I can usually find between ten and twenty of these. (In extremely hot markets where homes appreciate at double-digit rates, you shouldn't go back farther than a few months or so in order to prevent the CMA from being skewed downward.) Don't forget that the amenities and how nice a home looks will affect the curb appeal and salability of the property but have very little impact on appraised value, so it's best to use as many comparables as possible. In selecting my comps, I use the subdivision, the square footage (with a range of plus or minus 10%), and the number of bedrooms and baths. I then calculate the average sale price of the group, eliminating any outliers up or down (e.g. homes that were foreclosures or distress sales).

Finally, I pull up all the active comparable listings. Again, I use the subdivision, the square footage, and the number of bedrooms and baths, but *your* market may be a little different in how the appraisers select comparables. The point is to get as much data as possible!

Now we put it all together. Take the adjusted value from the tax records, add the average price from the closed comps, and then add the average price from the active comps. Now take that number and divide by three, and you'll have the true average value for the subject property. Write down this new number somewhere, add 5% and subtract 5% from it, and you'll have a "reasonable range" for the value of the home, which tends to be plus or minus 5% from the average. In most markets it's reasonably easy to support a value within

5%; so once the property sells, getting the appraisal shouldn't be an issue.

I know this is an out-of-the-box way of doing a CMA, but it will absolutely stand any amount of scrutiny by clients, other agents, or – most importantly – appraisers. Moreover, using this method will protect you from accidentally over-pricing or under-pricing a property. Most importantly, it will reinforce the fact that you're a market authority and know what you're talking about. If a seller client should be harboring a suspicion that you're trying to skew the numbers, his or her fears will quickly be allayed because you've considered every possible comparable in the current value of the home. Nothing except pre-appraisal could be fairer.

PUTTING THE PIECES TOGETHER

Now let's take the pieces and put them together into a "lethal" listing presentation. For quick review, what are the pieces?

1) Knowing your market statistics so that you're truly the best person for the job.
2) Knowing the value of the subject property so that you can get the top dollar for your seller client.

Beginning the process without laying this foundation simply won't work. It's absolutely critical that you go through the first two steps before you learn the listing presentation, simply because the presentation *builds on this foundation!* Without a suitable foundation on solid ground, you'll be building your presentation on quicksand and won't be able to list properties using my unique method. Why? Because you won't have the most important element of any sale: the believability factor. This approach is counter-intuitive, and, as such, it demands that you have credibility. If you don't have credibility, the listing approach will never sell because you're asking the client to place his faith in an approach that, in all likelihood, he's never heard of before.

TWO WAYS TO SELL THE HOUSE

There are more than 1.1 million REALTORS® in America, and I guess you could say that there are 1.1 million ways to sell a house. But the truth is that there are really only *two* ways to sell a house: you can sell it by price, or you can sell it by traffic. Every other sales method is a subsidiary of one of these two. We'll explore the two different approaches at length and discuss how they differ and how one of them will yield far better results for your client while making you more money.

1) The Price Approach, a.k.a. The Traditional Approach. I've read dozens of books – probably hundreds of books – on the subject of real estate. Many of these books speak of the importance of listing real

estate, and all of them describe nearly identical listing approaches, with only slight differences. Now, the reason for all this sameness is obvious: it's the way listings have been done since the beginning of real estate. It's the old "if it ain't broke, don't fix it" thing. Well, I'm here to tell you that it's broken! If you expect to make a lot of money in real estate, you need to determine what everybody else is doing and then do the opposite.

Okay, here's the basic formula for the "traditional" or "price" approach. As you'll recall, we talked earlier about building a CMA, or comparative market analysis, for your client. The traditional approach teaches us to find the "reasonable range" of value and then try to list the property on the low end of that range.

If the home doesn't sell within a month or so, we're all taught to...what? You got it! To ask for a reduction in price. Then if the property still doesn't sell, we lower the price again, and again, and again, until eventually we find a buyer for the place. Think about it: we're selling the house by *price*. We're using *the price* as our marketing tool. That's why we continue to lower the price, or wait for appreciation in the market to lower the price *for* us, until the house eventually sells.

One of the reasons this approach works well for the agent is that it places the entire burden of selling the home on the seller! Another reason for using the traditional approach is that the agent doesn't have to spend a lot of money marketing the house. He doesn't have to spend a lot of time or effort devising a marketing plan or promoting the property because the price is doing the selling for him. There's no doubt that this approach will work, of course: it's been working for decades with good and bad agents alike. However, there are a few drawbacks to the traditional approach that are seldom mentioned.

First and foremost is the agency issue. It's your job as the listing agent to represent the seller's interests, which include getting the absolute top dollar for the property. However, most agents *don't* get top dollar when they use this approach, and the reason is as simple as supply-and-demand. When there are fewer buyers competing for a home, the sale price may need to be discounted substantially in order to attract interest. In economics-speak, "with a fixed supply and a scarce demand [i.e. fewer buyers], prices drop."

Another drawback to using this approach is lack of speed: several months may pass before the traditional approach begins to have an effect. In the process, the home often becomes stigmatized. After several reductions, it's not even shown to potential buyers because it's been on the market "too long" and is now assumed to have something wrong with it. If the agent starts the process too high and then reduces the price too slowly, the home becomes very difficult to sell at any price.

Many times, listing agents unwittingly become de-facto buyer sub-agents; and even though I don't know a single listing agent who would knowingly sell out his client, it's entirely too easy with the traditional listing approach to help the buyer rather than the seller. And, yes, I realize that my judgment may sound harsh, but if you'll honestly examine this method, you'll have to agree that, very often, it doesn't yield the best results for the seller.

2) <u>The Traffic Approach</u>. To understand the traffic approach, we need to turn our attention again to the "reasonable range." Real estate is entirely different from liquid investments with absolute values. For instance, anybody can look up a share of stock and immediately see its current price. But because values are subjective in real estate, there tends to be about 10% flexibility in the price range. Consider a home that's valued at $100,000. It's not worth *exactly* $100,000! It's really worth between $95,000 and $105,000. If the price drops below $95,000, nearly everyone will agree that the house is a good deal; and if the price goes above $105,000, nearly everyone will agree that the property is priced a little too

high. However, within the "reasonable range" there is little price resistance.

Here's how the traffic approach works. Instead of listing the home at the low end of the range, you raise its price to the high end. The problem? Now there's no compelling reason for anyone to show it or buy it. Okay, here's the secret weapon: you raise the commission by 2%! What you're doing, effectively, is "bribing" agents to include your listing on their show lists. What *I* do is raise my commission from 6% to 8%, and then I raise the price about 10%. The client then nets about 8% more money before any negotiations!

Sometimes, not often, the appraisal knocks the price down some. When that happens, it's usually a minor adjustment, and then the seller has the option of lowering the price to match the appraisal, or the deal, as written, falls apart. The buyer also has the option of paying, out of pocket, the shortfall in the appraisal or canceling the deal if there's an appraisal contingency. When that happens, the client knows that he got the absolute top dollar for his home.

Now, I know that almost any REALTOR® will immediately say, "I never look at the commission when I'm working for a buyer." But I don't believe that noble-sounding claim because statistics clearly indicate that it's not true. I don't know any agent who would intentionally sell a buyer client a home that wasn't right for him; but if there are sixty homes in the market that generally match the client's criteria, and if three of those homes pay higher commissions than the rest, it's certainly not unethical to make sure that those three properties end up on every show list. In addition, there's nothing wrong with hoping that your client chooses to buy one of the three. If he doesn't, no big deal; but if he does, you just got a big bonus!

One of the questions I'm often asked is why I don't just offer a bonus to the selling agent. Once again, the answer is simple. Every buyer's agent knows that if he doesn't present a full offer, the first money to come off the table will be the selling bonus. Since most homes don't sell for full offers, the selling bonus doesn't happen very often, so the buyer's agent can find himself torn between not getting the bonus and not representing his client. If he advises his client to offer less than the listing price, he knows that his bonus is most likely gone. On the other hand, if he encourages the buyer to pay the listing price, he's probably not fully representing the buyer's interests. For that reason, the selling bonus is often a *dis*incentive rather than a legitimate incentive.

So now you have the theory behind my listing approach. Next you'll receive the presentation itself, and I believe you'll find it to be the most powerful listing presentation you've ever seen!

CHAPTER 4 —
MY LISTING PRESENTATION: WHAT TO SAY AND HOW TO SAY IT

<u>INSIDE CHAPTER FOUR:</u>

- WHAT TO SAY AND HOW TO SAY IT
- TAKING LISTINGS OVER THE PHONE
- REAL-LIFE EXAMPLES

Previously we focused on how to become the best agent for the job. We mentioned the necessity of learning market statistics, and how and where to find them. We discussed how you can increase your credibility and power by arming yourself with this basic and relevant knowledge. Next we determined the best way to build an accurate CMA, or comparative market analysis, and then we touched on the theory behind my listing presentation. If you've been studying the information, you know how and why this presentation works.

Now, in this chapter I will show you how to present my listing plan to a seller client. I ask you to read with pen or highlighter in hand, and to take notes. You should expect to review the material again and again until it has been fully absorbed. And if you do, I promise that you'll be listing properties at 8% or more – every time!

WHAT TO SAY AND HOW TO SAY IT

I want you to pretend that you're the listing agent in this story. It may not be a true story for you *yet*, but it could be. It's worked for me countless times.

Imagine that it's a Thursday morning. You've just come into the office and noticed a CMA request that arrived from your website overnight. If you're like most agents, that kind of good news doesn't happen often; but, in *my* case, not a day goes by that I don't receive one or two CMA requests from potential sellers – and all because of the technology that I use to capture traffic from my website.

But once again I'm getting ahead of myself. We'll discuss how to have an unending supply of listing leads, as well as buyer leads, in the next chapter. For now, let's stick with the listing presentation.

Okay. So it's Thursday morning, and you have a new CMA request in your inbox. The first things you do are to pull up the tax value and print out the tax sheet, which will tell you a lot about the property *and* the CMA request. Using the tax records and the appreciation rates for that area, you determine the approximate value of the home.

Next you log into your MLS database and pull up all the closed comparables for the seller's subdivision, with the approximate size and number of bedrooms and baths. There are twenty-one comparables to use and only one obvious distressed sale, so you eliminate that one from the average. After finding an average for the other twenty, you print out the comps in a one-liner format and note the "average" price on the page.

Next you pull up all the active comparables listed in the MLS (three, in this case), average them, print out the query, and write down the average price.

Now add the three prices that you've written down, and divide by three. Obviously, this is your average sale price. Multiply it by 5%, and add the amount to the average for the high end of your reasonable range. Then *subtract* 5% from the average to give you the low end of the range. In a matter of minutes, you've completed a very thorough CMA that's beyond scrutiny. That's a good first step.

So now you call the seller and thank him for visiting your website. You tell him that you received his home-valuation request and that you're in the process of compiling data to determine the home's value. *I* generally tell the seller that I've seen nice homes and bad homes, as well as some in the middle, and I'd like to know where, really, *his* home is. I ask him to pretend that I'm Stevie Wonder and to give me a verbal tour of the place, since I'm not actually there to view it.

I allow him to take me from room to room, all the while asking him for specifics about the home's curb appeal and other possible attractions. After touring the house, we next "go" outside, where I have him talk me through the yard, the exterior paint, the roof, the overall condition, the immediate neighbors' homes, and the landscaping.

Then I generally say something like, "Gosh, that sounds like a really nice house! Why on earth would you want to sell it?" The response I get is very important because it can provide me with the seller's motivation and, often, his time frame.

Trying to determine whether or not the seller has a realistic grasp of the situation, I then ask him if he has any idea what price should go on the house. Sometimes sellers aren't completely practical about these things (I bet you already knew that!), but generally they are. And if a seller *isn't* a realist, he will likely believe that his home is worth much more than the initial CMA would indicate. So then I proceed with something like this: "Wow! You must have a *really* nice home. I'm looking at every single house that's been sold in your neighborhood during the past year, and I'm not seeing anything within $15,000 of that price. Can you help me understand what features your home has that make it stand out so much?"

Many times he'll tell me that the house down the street sold for that much even though it isn't nearly as nice as his. Generally, however, the seller down the street just didn't want anyone to know he had to sell his house for much less than he'd been asking. But now that you have the comps in your hand, you can tell the seller *exactly* what a house sold for, and sometimes that little fact is all you need to introduce some reality into the situation. On the other hand, sometimes your potential client's home actually *is* worth more than you would've expected, so you also need to be open to what he tells you. On those rare occasions, you should be prepared to tweak your CMA a little.

Now that you know the seller's motivation, his time frame, and his opinion of the property's value (it *could* even be that he had a recent appraisal, which he's now using to test you), you can tell him that you'll complete your research and then call him back with your valuation. Simply set up an appointment, and either call or visit in person.

TAKING LISTINGS OVER THE PHONE

Yes, you read it right! In fact, I've taken roughly *85% of all my listings* over the phone! And you can do the same thing with this approach.

Okay, so you have the listing appointment and the information you need going in: the value of the home, the seller's motivation, his time frame, and his expectations. Now it's time to nail the presentation. Before we get into the actual interchange, though, let's talk about what the seller is expecting (and what virtually every other agent is gearing up to give him).

The seller's expecting you to come in and tell him how great his house looks. He's expecting you to tell him how terrific your company is (and it may be). He's expecting you to tell him how great an agent you are and how many zillion dollars' worth of property you've sold. He's expecting you to tell him his kids are cute. He's expecting you to tell him he needs to fix this and that. He's probably sold a house before, he's already talked to a REALTOR®, and/or he's talked to friends who've been through the process. So let's assume that he plans to interview several agents, as many sellers are doing nowadays.

The single most powerful thing you can do is surprise him. Remember: you want to look at what everyone else is doing, and then do the exact opposite. What do I mean? Other agents will talk about themselves. *You* need to talk about the seller. Other agents will extol the virtues of their companies, and in nebulous terms they'll explain how they plan to sell the house. *You* need to talk about different strategies for selling the house and then *show* the seller exactly what the process will mean to him in terms of DOM and selling price.

But back to the listing presentation. When you arrive at the home, quickly introduce yourself, and then tell the seller that you're very sorry, but you don't have a lot of time, and you want to make the most of what you *do* have. (He'll be thrilled because he's been expecting this ordeal to go on for hours!) Now, let's hope you get lucky and he says, "I'm talking to 'Agent X,' and he says he'll list the house for 5%. How much do you charge?"

At this point I'd tell the seller, without hesitation, "I try to get 100%" – and then I wouldn't say a word. After about ten seconds (which feels like an eternity!), he'll usually start laughing. Then I'll politely say, "Regardless of what anyone may tell you, there are two parts of selling your home that are completely under your control: the commission and the selling price. And what price and what commission you choose will largely depend on the type of strategy you decide to use. Do you know what I mean by that?" (Invariably he'll say no, which is perfect. What he's just now done is set me up!)

"Mr. Seller, here's what I mean. There are 1100 REALTORS® in our market, and I guess what that translates into is that there are 1100 different ways to sell your house. But the truth is that all those different approaches really boil down to just two different strategies: you can sell your house by price, or you can sell it by traffic. Does that make sense? (At this point, either he'll say no, or he'll guess wrong.) Well, here's what I mean. If you were to go to [name of the biggest local bookstore] and find the real estate section, you could see lots of different books on how to be a top agent. And each of those books would teach you one single way of selling houses. It's the 'traditional' approach, and nearly all the agents have used it for years. I call it 'the price approach' because it uses the price to sell your house.

"Here's what I mean by that. A house isn't like a loaf of bread or a share of stock. You can't go to the computer or call someone on the phone and get a price for it. The price on a house is much more subjective, and it's somewhere within a 'reasonable range.' Let's say, for example, that some imaginary house is worth $100,000. It's not actually worth $100,000, though; it's worth between about $95,000 and $105,000, depending on the motivations of the buyer and the seller. Now, if you start listing the price much over $105,000, everyone will pretty much agree that it's too high. And, by the same token, if the price drops down below $95,000, everyone will agree that it's a good deal.

"The way we've all been taught — what all of us real estate agents have been taught — is to convince you, the seller, to list your house at the low end of that 'reasonable range.' That way, the price can be used to motivate a buyer to write an offer. If the home doesn't sell in a month or so, we're supposed to go back to you and ask you to reduce the price, telling you that the market has spoken and that your house must not be worth as much as you'd thought. Then you agree to reduce the price, and we wait. In another month, if the house still doesn't sell, we reduce the price again. Eventually, we'll suck in some bottom-feeder who'll be happy to 'steal' your house.

"Now, there's nothing wrong with this approach. It will definitely sell your house, but it's an expensive way to go about it." This is when I generally pause for effect. Then I say, "But what I'd do if I were you is use another approach, or what I call 'The Traffic Approach.' If it were my house, we'd *raise* the price about 10%, to $105,000! And then we'd set aside about 2% to use as a 'bribe.' In other words, I'd raise the price 10% and the commission 2%. But let me explain. If we were to look in the MLS right now, you'd find about 300 or so homes with more or less the same size, features, etc., as your house. Now, when an agent has a buyer customer who's looking for that type of house, he's not going to show all 300 of them. Instead, to keep his broker happy, he'll probably show the client any homes listed by *his* company that happen to meet the criteria, but after that he'll probably choose to show only a few others.

"What this strategy will do is ensure that your home gets put on the show list. That's *all* it'll do... but it's enough. Here's why. I don't know of any agent who'd try to talk his customer into buying a house that wasn't right for him, simply to make a higher commission. But, on the other hand, I don't know of any agent who wouldn't *hope* for his client to choose the home that paid the best. REALTORS® are just regular people, and if they can make more money doing the same amount of work representing their clients, you can bet they will.

"Do you remember Field of Dreams? The famous line from that movie was, 'If you build it, they will come.' Well, in real estate, if you *bribe* them, they will come! The fact is that, in order for your home to stand out in a sea of other homes for sale, there must be something 'outstanding' about it. With the traditional approach, it's the price (if not immediately, then eventually) that makes the house stand out. But with the traffic approach, it's the abnormally high commission. It's really very simple."

Then I'd tell the seller that I'm equally comfortable using either approach (which I am), but I'd be less than honest if I claimed that the two methods had similar results. The fact is that, while using the traffic approach, we have historically sold our clients' homes in about half the time and *netted* them more money in the process!

REAL-LIFE EXAMPLES

Finally, I'd tell the seller of some cases where I've used the traffic approach and had great results. Remember: Jesus taught in parables. Why? Because people love stories. A story can take the vaguest idea and make it imaginable by making it real. Here are a few of my favorite stories that I've used countless times in the past.

Through my website, a client who was a licensed broker in Boone, North Carolina, approached me one day last year. His parents had passed away, and because of his real estate experience his siblings had chosen him to help sell the family home. So he called the largest company in our market, which happened to be Coldwell Banker, and listed the home for $64,900. Over the course of two years, Coldwell systematically reduced the price to $59,900. But even though it was a very nice little house, the seller hadn't received a single offer on it during the course of the listing contracts.

When I explained my idea to the broker, I could see the lights come on in his mind! As an agent, he intuitively knew that this approach would work, so at my suggestion we raised the price to $70,000 and the commission from 6% to 8%. (The co-op was half.) Well, within a month we had received three offers! The first two we turned down, but the third was a full offer, and we accepted it. Still, we had one more hurdle to get past: the appraisal had to support the sale price. As it turned out, the appraisal came in short, and my client had to sell the home for $69,500 and do some minor repairs that amounted to less than $600 (and probably would've had to be done with any sale at any price).

So after raising the price $10,100 and then paying an extra $1390 (the 2% extra commission), my client netted $8210 more money and got the absolute top dollar for his childhood home. Even more importantly, we accomplished in under ninety days what he'd failed to do in two full years: we got offers and were able to command the maximum price because of the traffic generated by the higher commission. Was he happy? He was ecstatic! And so was I.

Here's another story you'll love. Again, I had a client approach me through my website. (Are you noticing a trend here?) This fellow was very frustrated because he'd bought a brand new home, closed on it, and was having to make two mortgage payments every month. He'd tried to sell the home FSBO; and although he'd shown it a lot, no offers had materialized. Then he listed it with a local brokerage, but the home received no offers and had very few showings. After the listing expired, I went to see him and showed him my approach, and he decided to try it. We raised the price from $79,900 to $86,000, immediately had a surge of showing traffic, and, in exactly seven days, sold the home for the full price of $86,000. As in the previous story, we then anxiously waited for the appraisal, but this time it went through without a hitch. To this day, my client thinks that I'm a genius and sends me business every chance he gets.

So let's do the math on this one: the additional commission cost him $1720, the additional price he was able to command was $6100, and his net benefit was $4380, or over 5% more money! Best of all, the house sold almost immediately!

I could go on and on with these stories, but I'll share just one more. This client was one of those know-it-all people. I approached him with both options, as I always do. His initial reaction was that he'd never heard of the traffic approach and was skeptical because he had a problem with the high commission. So we initially listed the home at 7% (let me remind you that we're in a 6%-or-less market), and we waited. We had a slightly-better-than-average number of showings, but nothing outstanding and no offers for about four months. Eventually, though, the client began to get frustrated (not a new thing to many of you listing agents, I'm sure) and called me to ask what I thought he should do. He was in a hurry to sell the home and had a lot of equity, so he'd listed it for $146,000. I asked him if he remembered what I'd suggested when he first listed the house, and he said, "Not really."

Then I suggested that we raise the price to $156,000 and the commission to 8%. He'd been considering *reducing* the price and was naturally stunned when I told him to raise it. Well, we closed not long afterward! He was very thankful for my getting him top dollar, and I can promise you that he'll never sell another home the same old way. Quickly looking at the math, you can see that we raised the commission 1%, or $1560, and we commanded $10,000 more for the home and sold it almost immediately.

Now, did I do anything differently in any of those cases? Absolutely not! I advertise all of my listings exactly the same ways and show no preferential treatment, regardless of price, commission rate, or pressure from the client. What sold those homes and many more just like them was the commission.

But it gets even better! What's the first thing we're all taught to do when a home doesn't sell? That's right: *lower the price*. But what I generally do is convince my client to *raise the commission*. We've raised the commission as high as 12% to sell a home that otherwise would've sat vacant forever. It's amazing what a lot of showing traffic will do for even the worst dog of a house.

So there you have the listing presentation that's made me one of the top listing agents in the country and earned my clients and me lots of money. And now that you have the "ammo," in the next chapter I'm going to give you the "gun." In order for you to be a top listing agent (or buyer's agent, for that matter), there's one thing you simply must have: *an unending supply of new customers.* In the next chapter I'm going to share with you the technology I use to generate as many as seven listing leads every single day — and between fifty and seventy new buyer customers! The next chapter is one you won't want to miss.

CHAPTER 5—
GETTING BUSINESS TO COME TO YOU

INSIDE CHAPTER FIVE:

- THE SECRET OF MY SUCCESS
- GETTING BUSINESS TO COME TO YOU

I want you to imagine that you just got up out of bed and went to your computer to check your email. It's still early and dark outside, but you're getting ready for a full day. You look at your inbox and find twenty-three new leads there —people who visited your website overnight while you slept. I know: you think this is a dream. But it's *not* a dream. It's reality! And it could happen for you.

In the previous chapters we discussed what many agents believe to be the most powerful and unique listing presentation to come along in years. I know that I've used it to list as many as 114 homes in a single year—all at 8% or more. Also, because the system is so simple and makes perfect sense, I've been able to list about 85% of the properties over the phone, saving *me* countless hours and saving *my clients* the hassle of the at-home suppertime listing presentation.

Still, even the best listing presentation in the world is only as good as the number of opportunities you receive (and even the worst listing presentation is effective if you present it to enough sellers!). Using the traffic presentation, I've lost only two listings where I was able to present. But I could be really bad and still be the top listing agent in our market. Why? Because I receive *tons* of seller leads. I can't remember the last day when I didn't receive at least one. That's my secret weapon! I get many chances, and *because* I get those chances, I also get many listings.

THE SECRET OF MY SUCCESS

Okay. Now that you know my secret involves getting *lots of chances*, let me be more specific. I use three pieces of technology, together, to generate my business, both buyers and sellers. And it's the *way* that I use the components that helps me land and keep the business.

1) The first piece of the technology puzzle is my website.

   Now, I realize that I'm about to go against conventional wisdom in what I'm going to teach you, but in the three years that I've been doing Internet real estate, I've experimented with virtually every type of website available. I've used template websites, and I've built my own. Here's what I've learned.

When I started in this business, all the "experts" told me that content is king. They let me know that every successful website has to include mountains of content. So of course I set out to have every kind of content imaginable. I had school reports, local community information, and links to various community sites, such as the chamber of commerce, the visitors' bureau, local hotels and restaurants, the school board, and more. I had information about our city, our state, and my company. I had general relocation information. I had weather, news, sports, and human-interest content. I had every imaginable kind of financial information – from a couple of dozen financial calculators, to articles about mortgages and credit, to lender comparisons, to rates, to pre-qualification forms, to credit repair, and then some. In fact, I had literally *hundreds* of pages of real-estate-related content. I offered free reports. I offered listings by email and free CMA's.

After much testing and many changes, though, I learned (belatedly!) that content *isn't* king. I also learned that most of the "experts" don't have a clue about online real estate marketing, which is why most real estate websites look alike and generate very little business for their owners. Today I have what is probably the simplest website you've ever seen, and I receive an amazing number of customer comments about how nice it is to find a real estate website that's easy to use. You know, it's always wise to give consumers what they want, and I'm here to tell you that *simplicity* is what they're searching for. Nowadays, in terms of content, there are only three things on my website.

First and foremost, there's a link to my local MLS, using IDX (internet data exchange). This is not the private, or "for-REALTORS®," side of the MLS, but the public-access side. If you don't have it on your website, you absolutely must get it because 92% of all Internet real estate customers want to search for homes *on* the Internet. And if you don't have IDX available in your market, you need to insist that your local Board of REALTORS® make it available. In the meantime, there are several reputable companies that will build a custom IDX link for you at a reasonable cost. But if that solution is out of your budget, you should at least link to Realtor.com or one of the other sites that have large groups of listings.

Next, you should offer to send your visitors free listings by email. This very powerful tool gives you multiple excuses for contacting a buyer without making him feel "pressured." Almost any MLS application will allow you to input a customer's preferences into its system so that it can email him any new listings that meet his criteria. In most markets, this service is free to member agents. But if you don't have the automated system, it's still a good idea to offer the service, even if you have to pull up listings for your clients manually.

Finally, you should offer a free CMA (comparative market analysis). One of the first concerns that a seller will have is how much his or her home is worth, and many visitors will request a free CMA if one is offered. However, it's important that you not refer to it as a CMA because that's REALTOR® jargon, and most non-REALTORS® don't know what it means. You should use clear, self-explanatory terminology like "free market valuation" or "free home value" or "free house valuation" or anything else in plain, non-industry English that your visitor can understand.

Those three items and my contact information are absolutely all that's on my website now. Yet I have one of the most frequently visited websites and clearly the largest web presence in our local community, using only what I've just described. Remember the "KISS" rule? Keep it simple, Stupid! Well, this rule certainly applies to real estate websites: less is definitely more when it comes to attracting Internet customers.

(To view the Agent SimpleSite™ that we use, just go to: http://www.AgentSimpleSite.com.)

2) The second piece of critical technology is the <u>database, or CRM (customer relationship manager) application.</u>

There have been books written about the importance of having a database, not only as a customer management tool, but also as an asset to sell when and if you decide to retire from real estate. I don't think it's possible to overstate the importance of having and using a database.

Moreover, as you grow to become a higher-volume agent or top producer, you'll find it virtually impossible to maintain a significant level of transaction volume without using a database. Having tried most of the major databases out there (dBase, Filemaker Pro, Access, Outlook, Outlook Express, Act, Gold Mine, Salesforce.com, Top Producer, Top Producer 7i, Online Agent, Agent Office, Market Leader) and having managed a team of agents, all of whom work the same pool of leads and share the same information, I can attest that there's one fact more important than all the others: the best database is the one you *use*! I first read this statement when taking my e-PRO® certification training and still consider it the very best information on the subject. Besides, if it's not simple, agents won't use it.

After trying unsuccessfully (many times!) to persuade our team of agents to use different database applications, we finally decided to develop our own. What we noticed in using the major real estate databases was that, even though advanced functionality is "cool," it's largely wasted on 99% of all agents. We also noticed that we tended to hire the 99% instead of the 1%! So what we desperately needed was a database application with a *five-minute learning curve*...not a five-day, five-week, or five-month learning curve.

Besides that, we needed an application that could be shared by multiple users, and we needed that application to be useable from numerous computers at any given time (a feature for which most companies charge additional license fees). When our agents needed to use the database, it had to be available, regardless of the hour, the location, or the computer, so it definitely had to be web-based.

Being web-based meant that multiple agents using different computers could access the data at one time without installing new software. Additionally, if somebody in our office were to buy a new computer, there would be no time-wasting hassle while the application was being installed on the new computer.

One of the most important aspects of a good database is *website integration*, which means that, when a customer visits your website and registers or fills out a form, his or her information is automatically inserted into your database (and nobody in your office has to type it in!). Most of the better databases include this function.

Also critical to a top-notch database are follow-up tools such as template emails that can be modified on the fly, call-back scripts, activity scheduling, customer contact history, and financial tracking—all built into the database application. These features reduce hours of menial work to mere minutes, leaving an agent free to do what he or she does best: listing and selling real estate.

An essential feature of the database application that our company developed is our Agent Success Panel. With only a few keystrokes, it allows us to reverse-engineer a business plan for a new agent. We can input how much money he wants to net for the next year, his brokerage split, and the average transaction and average commission rate in our market; and, in seconds, the database will make all the necessary calculations to build a business plan: how many customers or leads the agent will need, how many transactions, what to budget for customer acquisition, how many calls to make each day, how many appointments to schedule — the Agent Success

Panel literally builds the new agent a business plan! Even better, it then tracks his progress with that plan, allowing him to remain motivated. This tool has saved us two or three hours with each new-team-member orientation, and the plan can be changed by the agent at any time... *and* the system will adjust to compensate for the new variables! Very cool.

(For an online demo of our database application, visit our website at: http://CRM.FavoriteAgent.com.)

3) The final and, without a doubt, most important piece of the technology puzzle is the <u>LCM™ Gateway</u>.

Very few people have heard of the Internet term LCM™, or "lead capture module." Although this technology is unique to our agency, it's beginning to be copied by some of the biggest companies in the lead generation space. If this is your introduction to LCM™, you'll actually find it to be amazingly simple. Here's what I mean.

Real estate websites, as a rule, capture fewer than 1% of all unique visitors – or about half the site conversions of the average B2C (business-to-consumer) website, which gets about 2%. Hold on a second, though. I just threw a lot of technical jargon at you, didn't I? Let me back up.

In the field of website development, there are many measurements (metrics) that are important to the webmaster and the site owner, including total visitors, total unique visitors, abandonment, etc. The most important metric of them all, though, is the conversion rate (CR), also known as capture rate. This is the percentage of unique visitors (first-time visitors, generally) who actually fill out the guest registration or online registration form. According to the experts who measure these statistics, real estate websites rate among the worst of all B2C websites in terms of site conversion, or CR.

The typical real estate site has a CR of less than 1%, which means that, of 100 unique visitors to a website, not even one actually registers or identifies himself. This is because real estate websites aren't designed to capture traffic; they're designed instead to deliver real-estate-related information to home buyers and sellers, and they're pretty good at it. However, because they're not designed to bring in customers, they generally don't!

Our LCM™ Gateway technology was designed to do only one thing: capture Internet traffic – and it does incredibly well at lead capture. Instead of 1%, or even the 5-6% that the very best real estate sites can do, our LCM™ Gateway routinely captures between 30% and 40% of all unique visitors! But how does it succeed so well? The answer to that question is in nearly three years of continual testing and improvement. Every little gain took weeks or even months of concentrated fine-tuning! What follows here are the basics (although much of the detail is beyond the scope of most webmasters, let alone REALTORS®, so don't despair if you can't immediately comprehend everything).

Most important: on your website, have a form in the path of the strongest value proposition. In fact, simply adding a form in front of the IDX link will bring your conversion rate up to 4-5%. Many agents are afraid to do so, however, because they think they'll lose people at this point...and they're right! "People" *will* leave. The *freeloaders* will leave – and I say good riddance! We're trying to earn a living here! Where is it written that a REALTOR® has to operate a charity? If a customer is unwilling to identify himself, I'm unwilling to share my IDX link with him. Let him go mooch off some other agent.

Other factors that effect the CR are colors, landing page content, advertising content, font size, font color, the order of the fields on the contact form, the number of fields on the form, the speed at which the pages load, the size and presence of images, the actual HTML, JavaScript, and ASP or PHP code (if any), and many other details. Suffice it to say that, if it were easy to get a high CR, everyone would have one.

Let's face it: if you're a webmaster or know a lot about site development, you could probably build a high capture rate into your website yourself, assuming that you were willing to spend thousands of hours in development over a period of two or three years. However, if the technology had been available when I started, I can assure you that I would've gladly bought it instead of developing it.

As it turns out, so many people called me asking for help on website lead capture that ultimately I decided just to license the technology to our agent partners. Therefore, if our development team chooses to partner with an agent, that person is allowed to use the finest lead capture technology available anywhere, regardless of price. Our site conversion rate is unequaled on any real estate website platform!

(To see our LCM™ Gateway technology in action, visit our website at:
www.LCMGateway.FavoriteAgent.com.)

GETTING BUSINESS TO COME TO YOU

Now that we've discussed the secret of my success and the specific technology solutions responsible for the volume of business that my company does, let's talk about how to get the business to come to you. What can you do to get visitors to your website? Are there some strategies that are better than others? What about SEO (search engine optimization)? What about PPC (pay-per-click) advertising?

Well, assuming that you've developed a good trap and that you've got a relatively good site conversion rate (CR), the next thing you need is a strategy to send the most customers to the site for the least amount of money. *How* they get to the site is much less important than *the fact that they get there*, but there *are* some things you should do to maximize your traffic and minimize the cost of that traffic.

First, put your web address on everything you do. Your yard signs, your business cards, your post cards and direct mail, any print advertising, such as home magazines and newspapers, any flyers or brochures that you're using in your marketing: all of these should have your URL, or web address. All of these should promote your website.

If you do any media advertising, you should mention your website several times in your message. Radio works well in markets where you can afford it, as does TV and, in some markets, the Real Estate Channel. Make your website part of your brand!

If you use a call-capture hotline system or Auto Attendant on your phone system, be sure to mention your website in any voice mailbox or greeting. On-hold music can include references to your website and the benefits of shopping online for houses.

Finally, there's the whole area of paid traffic. Paid-for traffic really comes in two varieties: direct and indirect.

Direct traffic is pay-per-click (PPC) advertisements or sponsored links in various search engines. The best three sources for PPC advertisements are Google, which includes – among other destinations – Earthlink, Ask Jeeves, and AOL; Overture, which includes Yahoo, MSN, AltaVista, InfoSpace, and CNN; and FindWhat, which includes CNET's Search.com, Excite, Webcrawler, MetaCrawler, Dogpile, and Microsoft Internet Explorer Autosearch. The key to using direct traffic is that it's performance-based, meaning that you pay only for results. You're charged only for traffic that comes to your site. If your site is able to capture at an effective rate (in other words, if your CR is high enough), direct is likely the best avenue for buying traffic.

Indirect traffic includes the whole field of search-engine optimization, or SEO, which involves hiring a firm to "chase" the search engine bots. To boost your site's natural ranking in the search engines, most SEO companies would use artificial means, including key word spamming, reciprocal linking, mirror page generation, and many other "gimmick" methods of tricking the search engine bots into thinking that your site is more relevant than it truly is. Of course, there are advantages and disadvantages to this type of traffic generation. One advantage is that, after you get your site optimized, you generate lots of traffic, and there's no additional cost for each visitor. A drawback is that the search engine algorithms change constantly in their attempts to stay at the head of the SEO industry. Their livelihood depends on their being able to provide relevant searches to their users, so they must filter out the "trick" methods of ranking. Google is very aggressive in this area, and, as a result, it continues to gain market share in the Internet search space.

The point of all this frenetic activity is that, for SEO to be effective in generating traffic, it has to be constantly run and continually monitored, and there's a price for everything! So the bottom line is that, if you're going to see any real amount of web traffic to your website, you're going to spend money directly in pay-per-click advertising, or you're going to spend it indirectly in search-engine optimization

Currently, we use PPC advertising through Google and Overture (as well as some minor SEO strategies that our own tech department handles), but we've spent thousands of dollars on SEO and used many different PPC sources in the past. Our method is to buy as much traffic as we can get from the cheapest sources. When we've generated all the business that we can handle, and then some, we scale back the ad buy.

Obviously, there are many good sources of advertising, but what *you* do, really, will come down to calculating your cost per lead (CPL). By using home-magazine ads in conjunction with a call-capture hotline and Internet marketing, we've generated more than two thousand new inbound leads per month. However (and most importantly), we've always used lead capture technology so that we could evaluate the cost per lead for each ad source. We treat advertising like an employee: it must be accountable for results, or we'll replace it. Very simple! And, by handling things this way, we're able to generate thousands of low-cost leads every month while keeping our marketing costs under budget. That's the secret of *getting business to come to you*.

In the next chapter we'll discuss the nature of Internet real estate and how it differs from traditional real estate. You'll learn how to work Internet leads and actually turn them into closed transactions. This is another chapter you won't want to miss!

CHAPTER 6— HOW TO TAP THE INTERNET EFFECTIVELY

INSIDE CHAPTER SIX:

- **TODAY'S AGENTS MUST TAP THE WEB**
- **AN INTERNET ADVERTISING PRIMER**
- **INTERNET REAL ESTATE FOR DUMMIES**
- **USING TECHNOLOGY TO GAIN SHARE IN A CROWDED MARKET**
- **I'M JUST LOOKING!**

In the previous chapters we've discussed how to become a listing expert and how to list homes at 8% or more every time. We've included information on how to get lots of listing customers, and we've shared various ways of acquiring an unending supply of buyer and seller leads. We've talked a little about technology-based real estate and the move that's sweeping our industry. Now it's time to discuss whether Internet real estate is for you.

TODAY'S AGENTS MUST TAP THE WEB

You read it right. Today's agents *must* tap the web! *This is not an option.* I must admit it: I don't like change, and the last thing I want to do is learn some new technology. But the fact is that 92% of all our customers are using the Internet for at least some part of their home searches, and that number is growing every year. To be out of the Net is to be out of business! Without the web, the lead aggregators are going to capture these leads before we can get them.

Here are some things you may want to know about Internet customers:

1) They're better educated.
2) They have more money.
3) They're buying more house.
4) Their search time is shorter.
5) They like to help in the process.

Sound like the perfect customers, don't they? While I think it's great to maintain your sphere of influence (SOI) and continually add previous customers to your group, most experts will tell you that referral business has fallen off across the country.

Why? Because, as a society, people today tend to be more transient than ever before. With the prevalence of corporate and military transfers, the idea of growing up and living your entire life in one community is no more than a dream or a distant memory for most Americans. And, since television and movies have replaced neighborhood activities, people are actually less social than ever before. These rather sad but realistic factors have incrementally reduced the effectiveness of network-based strategies such as SOI marketing.

Today's real estate customer is more demanding than his predecessors and wants information *right now*. Tomorrow's not good enough! He goes to the Internet to get that information, and if you're not there, several national lead aggregators *will* be there to grab him. It's imperative that you have a strong web presence, that you learn how to capture business from the web, and, most importantly, that you know how to respond to today's Internet customer.

AN INTERNET ADVERTISING PRIMER

The cost of traditional advertising has grown so dramatically that it's nearly impossible to keep your marketing expenditures within allowable limits. Let me explain. Experts tell us that real estate professionals should allocate no more than 20% of their GCI (gross commission income) to customer acquisition or advertising. Specifically, in a market where the average home price is $200,000, an agent shouldn't spend more than $600 in customer acquisition to produce the deal.

But here's what I mean. Let's assume for the sake of this illustration that the commission side is 3% and the agent/brokerage split is fifty/fifty. The gross commission generated for a single transaction would be $6000, the gross commission income to the agent (after brokerage split) would be $3000, and 20% of that $3000 is $600, which of course would be the absolute maximum an agent should spend on customer acquisition. But can you afford to spend that much on each lead? Certainly not. According to the national average, 24 leads are required to produce one transaction. So if you divide $600 by 24, your maximum cost per lead would be $25. Now, you don't necessarily have to spend $25 per lead, but you should definitely eliminate any source with a cost per lead of $25 or more. It doesn't matter if the ad salesperson is really nice or if several of your friends enjoy seeing your postcards. If you're spending more than $25 to produce a single lead, you need to eliminate it. Of course, each market has its own average home price, and each agent has a unique split arrangement with his or her broker, so you should adjust the math in the example above to fit your individual situation.

A typical one-edition magazine ad produces between ten and twenty leads for a full-page ad insertion. If the magazine ad costs $500 and you get twenty leads, you're staying in your budget (barely) —but if a $500 ad yields fewer than twenty leads, you need to eliminate it.

Postcard (direct mail) campaigns cost about $0.35 per unit, or $350 per thousand, excluding the time needed to do the mailing. The typical response rate for direct mail is 0.5% nationally, so the cost per lead is about $70. (1000 x 0.5% = 5 leads; $350/ 5 = $70 per lead.) If this equation doesn't make sense to you, go back and do the math again, and I'm sure you'll catch on pretty easily.

You should always evaluate each advertising source the same way, as in "How much money does this lead cost me?" Then you should advertise accordingly, depending on the number of leads you must get in order to generate the level of business you want to do. What I've found for our business is that Internet advertising is by far the cheapest and most scalable source of advertising, and it produces a more desirable customer as well. And what's even better is that we rarely have a cost of over $5 per lead for our advertising! That's because 1) we have an incredibly efficient capture device (our LCM™ Gateway technology), and 2) we're very stingy with our Internet advertising spending. Since we can generate customers for as little as $1.50 each, it's only natural that our business has evolved into one of the largest companies in our market in such a short time. We have a huge advantage over competitors who are spending $50 to $100 or more per customer. We can spend the same money and get 30-100 times as many results, simply by using this strategy and our technology! (To view a demo of our LCM™ Gateway technology, go to this link: http://LCMGateway.FavoriteAgent.com.)

INTERNET REAL ESTATE FOR DUMMIES

Let's assume that you've acquired either our technology or another Internet capture system to use with your website. Let's also assume that the system is integrated with your database so that follow-up is simple and seamless. In a few minutes, we'll discuss a typical follow-up scenario, but first we need to talk about the nature of Internet leads. How are they different from other leads, such as referrals or duty-desk leads? Should you handle them much as you would sign calls? Or should you treat them like open-house leads? How can you know how to approach them? Are they all the same?

The Real Estate Buying Cycle

A REALTOR® who has come up doing traditional real estate and who's been very successful at it is frequently unsuccessful when he tries to transition to Internet leads. Why? Because he tends to approach Internet leads the same way he's always approached leads, and for the first time in his career he'll find himself failing.

The first temptation for a confident and successful REALTOR® is to assume that Internet leads are of poor quality (since – for whatever reason, and even though he clearly knows how to prospect – he's not making a connection with these leads). This problem is compounded by the fact that many of the sellers of Internet leads provide very little information about them – often just a name and an email address.

The reason for the agent's failure in prospecting Internet leads is generally a fundamental misunderstanding of the real estate buying cycle. The Internet customer is a standard customer, with the same needs and motivations as any other real estate customer, except that (as research shows us) the Internet customer is the cream of the crop, so to speak. So let's talk about the real estate buying cycle and how we can use our knowledge to change the way we approach and follow up with real estate customers on the Internet.

The real estate buying cycle consists of three phases: information-gathering, the search, and finally escrow. The successful writing and acceptance of an offer-to-purchase mark the end of the search phase. Of course, there's still the escrow phase, which ends at closing. This buying cycle has been relatively unchanged for many years. Until recently, though, very few agents knew of the existence of Phase One. Make no mistake: Phase One has been with us for as long as people have used REALTORS® to buy real estate, but until recently it has remained largely unknown.

Phase One: Information-Gathering

The best research indicates that home shoppers begin the process of buying a house about 4-6 weeks before the beginning of Phase Two, or 6-8 weeks before the beginning of Phase Three. At first they're just thinking and dreaming, but that dreaming leads to visualization as they become obsessed with the idea of getting a new home. In fact, in their minds they've already bought one!

During the early part of Phase One, the buyer is thinking about budget, features and amenities, neighborhoods, and school districts. Let's not forget that this is the American Dream! We're taught from earliest childhood that home ownership is very much a mark and measure of success in our culture, so we want to be careful and thorough in our search process. In this initial phase, the customer is solidifying, in his own mind, what he wants to buy. He chooses his search criteria and his budget (often incorrectly, as any experienced REALTOR® can tell you!).

This is a very important part of the buying cycle, and it's going to happen whether we like it or not. The best thing we can do is realize it, accept it, and plan for it. Most importantly, Phase One of the buying cycle is the only part of the process that every customer wants to do on his own. Our clients don't want to have their dreams shaped by REALTORS®, parents, friends, or anybody else. They want the dream to be theirs. This phase is going to last 4-6 weeks. Anyone attempting to speed up the process does so at his own peril!

Phase Two: The Search

After the information-gathering phase has run its course, the buyer proceeds to a new phase and a mental shifting of gears. He's decided what it is that he wants and is now on a legitimate quest to find it. This phase typically lasts about two weeks, and, according to the NAR, the search process has actually been shortened by about a week during the last several years because of all the technology tools that are now available everywhere.

Real estate shoppers understand that they need us to help them in the process of finding their dream homes. In fact, the relative floundering of fee-based and discount brokerages suggests that our real estate customers do want us to help and are willing to pay us for our expertise. But what they *don't* want – and I can never reiterate this enough – is for us to try to shape their dreams. That part of the process is very personal for most customers.

During the search phase (Phase Two) of the buying cycle, the customer wants to look at actual houses.

He'll typically do lots of drive-by looking on his own and will begin skimming through home magazines. Remember: he now knows what he wants and is out to find it. And, somewhere in the middle of this search phase, he wants to begin working with a REALTOR®.

This is the crucial part of understanding the buying cycle: *the agent who's on the customer's mind when he reaches Phase Two is the agent who'll close the transaction and collect the commission!*

So how do you become *that* agent? (This is the secret to working Internet leads, by the way.) By being there! You need to be there at the precise moment when the prospective buyer calls a duty desk, the moment when he picks up a home magazine and calls an agent, the moment when he's out riding around looking at neighborhoods and decides to make a sign call. *This is how most agents have traditionally picked up their new customers!* The customer hasn't changed with the advent of the Internet. What *has* changed is *when* the customer comes into our lives; and this search phase, which is usually only two weeks long now, lasts until the customer finally finds his dream home and gets an accepted contract.

Later in this chapter I'll discuss some strategies that can help make you *the first REALTOR® your customer thinks of to call* when he reaches the critical transition point. But before I do that, and for the sake of continuity, I need to discuss with you the third and final phase of the buying cycle.

Phase Three: Escrow

Beginning with the acceptance of the contract and moving forward to closing, there's the third and final phase of the buying cycle, also known as the escrow phase. At this point, the buyer has found a home and is very emotional about it. Every little bump in the road becomes a drama, and this is one of the reasons that home buyers and sellers need us: we aren't emotionally connected to their dreams. Certainly, we identify with the client and wish the best for him — and let's not forget that we want to be paid for our work – but we don't have the level of emotional attachment to the transaction that our client feels.

Therefore, a skilled REALTOR® will minimize potential bumps in the road by making sure (in Phase Two) that the client has actually been pre-approved, not just pre-qualified. By the way he negotiates the contract, he'll show the client how to eliminate deal-breakers. He won't allow a home inspection to create needless drama but instead will utilize it only to protect the client from unseen structural damage in the house, rather than using it as a second negotiation round, as many beginning agents do.

How well Phase Three goes is entirely dependent on how well the agent does in Phase Two. It should be noted that almost all of the legal problems arising in real estate transactions will surface during Phase Three, which is why all of us need to excel at the setting and managing of customer expectations.

USING TECHNOLOGY TO GAIN SHARE IN A CROWDED MARKET

This is one of the most important things you can take away from reading my book. If you learn nothing else, you should at least be looking at Internet leads differently, and here's why. (Drum roll!) *Internet leads come during Phase One!*

Do you see the advantage? Has the light clicked on? Has the "Aha!" popped into your head yet? According to the National Association of REALTORS®, 74% of all buyers and 76% of all sellers will work with the first REALTOR® they talk to. What that statistic means, unfortunately, is that our clients see all of us as largely the same. We know that we *aren't* all the same, but what's important is what our clients think. If they see us as a commodity and more or less interchangeable, and if we still want to have some kind of strategic advantage, we need to be *first*. If we're first, the odds of our doing the deal are 3:1 in our favor. Period. The only way to change that ratio is to screw it up!

What a huge advantage! A smart REALTOR® will simply identify the customer first and then devise strategies to make sure that he doesn't screw up the process, so to speak. The rest will take care of itself. So let's talk about some of those strategies.

I'M JUST LOOKING!

I want you to think back to the last time you shopped in your favorite department store. Now, if you're like me, you don't have a lot of time to waste; when you go shopping, you go because you want to buy something.

But remember how, as you walked into the clothing department, a sharp sales clerk came up to you and said, "Can I help you?" (Oh, I'm sure that's never happened to you!) Now, I want you to be completely honest. What was your answer? You know what it was; it was the same as mine: "No, thanks. I'm just looking." And I'm willing to bet that, within five minutes, you were looking around and finding that same clerk to help you locate something in your size.

Did you really mean that you weren't interested, or were you implying that you wanted to gather information for a few minutes and that, later on, when you were searching, you might actually need his assistance? The procedure is no different for a real estate customer except that the buying cycle is much longer, given the price point of the purchase. The Internet customer is still gathering information when most agents call to say, "Can I help you?"

There are two reasons that an agent will fail in working Internet leads: either he'll take the "No, thanks. I'm just looking" literally, as though the customer wants nothing to do with him, *or* (more often) he won't take the hint and instead insists on trying to set up an appointment to start showing houses – immediately! This overbearing, hard-sell approach simply alienates the agent from the potential customer and removes any chance of his gaining the business. But make no mistake: that customer will go on to buy or sell, but *with another agent*. What a tragedy.

So how do we solve this fundamental problem? The first step is to accept the buying cycle and know that customers won't want us around much during Phase One. The next step is to have in place a follow-up system that will allow us to maintain contact with "future" customers over a longer period of time, even when we're feeling overwhelmed with "present" customers.

And that brings us back to having a CRM database application. The system that we license is designed to make the job as easy as possible. Here's what I mean: let's imagine that you're sitting at your desk, working on some prospecting or lead follow-up. It's, say, 7:00 PM, and a brand new lead drops into your database. As it turns out, a customer in California found out just today that he's being relocated to your market. So he got on the Internet and did a Google search for "your town real estate," and guess whose name appeared at the top of the page? That's right – yours did! So the customer looked at your information, liked the idea that he could search all the area listings using the MLS database, and then clicked your ad. That click cost you $0.87. Then the customer was routed to your LCM™ Gateway and was captured and inserted into your Agent CRM Database application in real time.

As you open the lead, you see that the customer has filled out a request to receive new listings by email. The notification email comes in within two minutes; so, being the good REALTOR® that you are, you immediately pull up the search criteria on the MLS and sift down through a preliminary cross-sectional list of various areas in your town. Next you click a couple of buttons to send the customer an email confirming his request for listings, and within five minutes you have him on the phone. You begin to engage him in a very low-key, non-pressure chat (reading a script that we've built into your database); and, before you know it, you're in a twenty-minute conversation about his plans, how nice your town is, etc. You really hit it off, and by the time you hang up the phone, you've told him that you'll be happy to find a good agent local to his area who will help him sell his existing home, with no guesswork. He's very appreciative, and you say goodbye after agreeing to touch base in a few days.

Next you post the notes from the call in your client record and then schedule yourself an activity for two days out. You plan to drop the new customer a note to tell him you'll be calling him the following day to update the listings you've been sending him. You then schedule the call in your database and put it out of your mind until it comes up on your activity calendar.

Next you call a few agents local to his area and interview them so that you can find a good referral agent. Then you give that agent the customer's info, and you let your client know that you've referred the agent. You stay in touch with the customer for about four or five weeks, sending him listings and community information and then making plans to meet him at the local airport when he comes in to shop. By now, though, his $375,000 home is under contract, netting you a referral fee of $2812.50 on the listing side for a few phone calls and a good lead.

In a matter of weeks your client flies to town, finds the home of his dreams, and buys it from you for $425,000, earning you a gross commission of $12,750 on the buyer's side. Since we're dreaming here, though, we'll also dream that the home he bought was one of *your* listings, gotten from the very same website—another lead that cost you $0.87 and some follow-up time. And since this *is* a dream, let's say that you listed the dream home using the listing strategy that I taught you, and the commission was 8%.

Oops! We need to recalculate the figures! At 4% per side, the commission earned on this listing is $17,000 *per side*! So let's total it all up:

```
    $17,000.00 commission (listing side)
 +   17,000.00 commission (buyer side)
 =   34,000.00 earned commission
 +    2812.50 referral for the other end
 = $36,812.50 total commission income
```

All this for a marketing cost of $1.74 plus a couple of months' technology lease! Your follow-up was seamless and simple, and the technology made you look really good. Did it make you a better agent? Not really. But it allowed you to maximize your potential as an agent. And, of course, the $36.8K didn't hurt either!

This is the power of information, technology, and the Internet. Before anyone else even realized there was business to be had, you had swooped in and captured it! Sounds too good to be true, doesn't it? But it's not!

This is exactly how, in under three years, I built my business from a single-agent practice to a company with nearly forty agents: by having lots of business—business before my competitors even knew it was out there! And I maximized my ability to service that business by leveraging my time with technology. As wild as this story seems, it could literally be you on a regular basis. It's me! And, before you know it, you'll have too much business to handle all by yourself, and you'll have to start feeding other agents. Maybe you'll begin to grow a team, and then you'll leverage your own efforts and multiply your time.

It's actually not uncommon for our agent partners to have to build teams to handle the volume. Some begin to build in a matter of weeks! Again, this isn't a dream; it's reality! And it can be *your* reality if you're up for the challenge and if you put the proper pieces in place. There's no reason for an agent to be struggling these days, considering the enormous advantage that the Internet can give you.

In the next and final chapter we'll discuss building a team, how the different team models work, and how to choose the model that's right for your business, depending on your growth and earning goals. This is the chapter that will really help you take your practice from doing thirty to fifty or so deals a year to doing hundreds, and of course you won't want to miss it!

CHAPTER 7 — TAKING YOUR BUSINESS TO THE NEXT LEVEL: BECOMING A RAINMAKER

<u>INSIDE CHAPTER SEVEN:</u>

- HOW TO BUILD A TEAM
- WHEN TO MOVE TO MANAGEMENT
- CLOSING THOUGHTS

During the previous chapters, we've discussed 1) the ultimate listing presentation that I've used to list 114 homes in one year at commission rates of 8% or more, 2) how to get more business than you can possibly handle for only a few dollars per lead, rather than spending hundreds of dollars for only a few leads though print advertising, direct mail, and lead generation companies, 3) the key technologies an agent must have in order to tap the Internet effectively, and, in our "Internet for Dummies" segment, 4) the new Internet agent.

I hope you've enjoyed all the previous chapters, and I hope they'll help you list and sell more real estate than ever before. As you know, these simple strategies and techniques have helped *me* build my company, in under three years, from a single-agent practice to a team of nearly forty members. This year alone, we expect to close 900 transactions and do an amazing 11% market share in our local market. If all goes well, we should net more than one million dollars in a market where the average sale price is only $126K.

I hope that you're now on your way to seeing your business explode, just as I did. However, tremendous progress creates a completely new series of problems. How do you assimilate all the growth? How can you get the most out of your newfound technology advantage? How can you build your business in a way that it can become larger than *you*? Is it possible to work smarter without working harder? What exactly are the different team models in use today? These complex questions bring us to the final chapter of this book: "Taking Your Business to the Next Level: Becoming a Rainmaker."

HOW TO BUILD A TEAM

Having had the privilege of working with hundreds of agents across the United States and Canada, I've seen many different types of business configurations. And, today, one of the primary real estate catchphrases is "team building," which seems to be the talk of every brokerage. How do we deal with teams? What constitutes a team? What are the brokerage's responsibilities and liabilities with a real estate team? How can I encourage teams in my brokerage without going broke? Since further questions are arising every single day, we'll begin dealing with them by defining the three basic "team models."

Rainmaker-Assistant(s) Team

This is the model of teamwork that's been around the longest, so we'll cover it first. Somewhere in the progression of an agent's business, he begins to hit a "ceiling" of production. That's a difficult thing to translate into dollars and cents, but it generally happens somewhere around forty or fifty transactions per year (or nearing one per week). The ceiling may be closer to fifty if the agent is extremely organized or closer to forty if he's not.

Another factor that affects the exact moment of contact with that ceiling is the agent's tolerance for less-than-excellent customer service. In other words, the more comfortable an agent is with "dropping the ball," the higher he can push the ceiling (and the longer he can delay contact with it – for a while!). Nevertheless, in nearly every case there's a production ceiling in the range of one deal per week, or maybe a bit less than that. For a top producer to push beyond the productivity ceiling, he *has* to hire an assistant or assistants.

The primary function of these assistants is to handle the administrative load associated with a high-volume practice, or to "put out fires" after the fact, or both. The rainmaker-assistant(s) team is the most common model, and it's good for increasing the agent's production maybe 20-30%, but nothing beyond that. Using this model, there's an *absolute* ceiling in the sixty-to-seventy-deal range, and adding *more* assistants actually increases costs and chaos. Other disadvantages related to this model are the high turnover rate of assistants and the very significant fact that they're a fixed cost on the top producer's business, as opposed to a variable cost. Why? Because assistants need to be paid every week, whether deals are closing or not. Generally speaking, they're employees, not contractors, and they're paid salaries. In the other models explained below, the addition of personnel is a variable cost — meaning that, if there's no volume, there's no cost.

The Support-Group Team

This odd phenomenon seems to be gaining popularity. In this model, several medium-producing agents from the same company will share duties and responsibilities so that they can have additional freedom. For example, one team member may pull another's floor duty or meet with a client so that the other member can go out of town for the weekend. Then a week later, they may very well switch places. This model is typically an alliance of equals and is used more for convenience and freedom than for leverage of production. In this model, each agent has his own relationship with the broker-in-charge, and each is treated as an individual with regard to agent splits, fees, and management. Most frequently, a support-group team consists of two agents, but occasionally it may grow to include four or five similarly producing agents.

The Leverage Team

The leverage team is the model that I recommend for the building of one's business. Here's how it works.

This team consists of one super-producer, or rainmaker, who produces more business than he can handle, so he recruits another licensed agent to work some of the overflow business. This recruit typically works on a split with the top producer, as set forth in a written team agreement. He's managed, trained, and given business by the rainmaker as well. The top producer has a relationship with the broker-in-charge; and, even though all the agents hang their licenses under the brokerage and the broker-in-charge, they're managed and paid by the top producer.

All corrections and communications flow through the rainmaker, and the production and the money are usually given to him. It's then the rainmaker's responsibility to disburse to subordinate agents according to the written team agreement. This model is essentially a company within a company and is the type of team that I built when I began to generate more business than I could handle.

The leverage-team model also allows for an agent to move to significantly higher levels of production because he's multiplying *time*. Top producing team leaders usually begin by handing out most of the buyer business to buyers' agents while continuing to do the listing themselves, simply because the listing side is more closely linked to lead generation. However, there's no hard-and-fast rule regarding the division of clients.

WHEN TO MOVE TO MANAGEMENT

In this type of team structure, the team is able to grow to about four or five agents before management responsibilities begin to overwhelm the rainmaker. If the team leader doesn't make the transition to management, he or she is destined to stall at this level. Depending on the team split agreed to, this first income ceiling is about twice the income that the rainmaker was able to make before starting the team. Here's the critical step:

> *To go to the next level, the agent must quit being a producing agent on the team and become the team leader full time. This change immediately cuts his income in half during the interim period, and most top producers don't want to sacrifice the short-term revenue. However, if the agent is willing to forgo the immediate gratification and invest in building the team, before long this team can be built to whatever level the top producer can support through the business he's able to generate.*

At this time, my team is nearing forty agents, and I haven't done a real estate transaction in a year and a half! This year I will make a seven-figure income from my brokerage while paying a full-time broker-in-charge to manage my team. In the day-to-day operations I'm involved only minimally, in some training and planning. Most of my work is devoted entirely to growing the national team, which already exists in more than over 500 markets. By the end of the year, we'll have more than 75 agents on the team, and we'll close 900 transactions. Most importantly, I won't be involved in *any* of these transactions. My situation is the ultimate in duplication of time, or leverage, and will make it possible for an agent to build his team as large as his imagination will allow.

So what's required to take a team to this level? Primarily, all you need is the vision to do it and the ability to generate an unending supply of inexpensive leads to feed your team. And to generate those leads, you simply have to have the technology in place; the rest is just a matter of putting more ad dollars to work in generating traffic to the technology. I've generated more than 2000 leads per month for over six consecutive months, all for a cost of between $1.50 and $4.00 per lead. Using our technology, my business is entirely scalable, and I don't have to spend money to generate additional leads until I've built the infrastructure to support that volume.

I use a rule-of-thumb of 24:1 to calculate how many leads I need to generate. What this means is that, if my agents are able to handle, on average, two deals per month, per agent, then I need to produce 1920 leads. (24 leads x 2 deals per month x 40 agents = 1920 leads.) And, from a management standpoint, I should hold each agent accountable for the leads that I refer to him. If his "deal rate" rises above 24:1, I need to find out why. I can easily identify problem areas in my team's prospecting and customer follow-up by monitoring deal rates.

Another number that I look for is a "reach rate" of 50%. (Any agent should be able to engage at least half of his customers in meaningful dialogues.) I also look for a 6:1 appointment rate, or one appointment for every six customers whom an agent reaches and begins to work with. Finally, I look for two appointments per transaction, or a ratio of 2:1. I want to see one closed transaction for every two appointments with a customer.

If the reach rate is too low, then I know that I have problems in the areas of discipline and prospecting. If the reach rate is good but the appointment rate is low, some basic sales training may be in order. Sales skills are developed, not inherited, and part of my job as a team leader is to help my team develop these skills. If an agent has a good appointment rate but a poor closing rate, he's probably making too many appointments with customers who aren't adequately pre-qualified. If I need to provide training for an agent so that he or she can better pre-qualify clients, that's what I'll do.

As you can see, at this level your job will be that of diagnostician and trainer-mentor. And it's fun! Nothing's quite like the feeling you get when you see dozens of transactions coming through from all the agents on your team – while you're taking the weekend off! This is what teamwork is all about: the multiplying of time for you, the rainmaker.

In summary, the possibility of building a mega-team comes down to a few key issues.

> First, you need to be able to create an unending supply of leads for your team. This goal is best

accomplished by having a very efficient capture technology, such as the LCM™ that we've developed.

Second, you need to have a common database that your team can use for following up on leads quickly and efficiently. At the same time, the follow-up notes and working notes need to be available for all the teammates to read, without interfering with the actual follow-up process.

Finally, you need to have the ambition to grow your business as large as it can grow. Can you see yourself as the leader of the largest team or company in your local market? If not, why not? Someone has to be the dominant agent in your city! Why shouldn't it be you?

CLOSING THOUGHTS

Well, this should give you some things to think about! If you apply the truths and principles in this book, you can literally turn your business around! You can actually become the dominant agent in your market in only a couple of years.

However, to do any job, you always need the tools. Don't worry, though: the tools in this case are very inexpensive and easy to use. It's just that they require a leap of faith. It's tough to spend money, sometimes money that you don't have, to sow the seeds of success for your business. Sometimes you have to make that leap. Sometimes you need to muster the courage to do what you know in your heart is right, even if your friends — even if your *broker* – never heard of *anything like* what you're doing.

Sometimes the first step toward being the leading agent in your market is simply...*leading*.

AFTERWORD

I challenge you to spend some time reviewing our website to see if our systems might be a good fit for you. We haven't yet selected all of our agent partners, and we'd love to talk to you. Remember: our agent partners have access to the same technology that we developed and that we're using every day for our local team. If you're interested, please call us toll-free at (888) 227-6856, or visit our website. If time isn't a problem, take the slow tour at http://About.FavoriteAgent.com.

On the other hand, if you're pressed for time and would prefer the condensed version, you can visit: http://Quick.FavoriteAgent.com.

If you visit the "Quick" site, you really ought to listen to my interview. Then feel free to browse around the site, and check out any or all of it.

As a first-time author, I'd very much appreciate your feedback. If you find this book to be helpful, or if some parts don't make sense to you, or if you have questions, please feel free to contact me.

My phone number is 1 (888) 227-6856, and my website is: http://FavoriteAgent.com.

Again, thanks for reading my book. The information that I've included here means a lot to me, and I hope that it will benefit you as well.

Matt Jones
President, CEO
REALTOR®, BROKER, ePRO®
FavoriteAgent.com

LCM: The Secret to Success in the New Age of Real Estate by Matt Jones is a FavoriteAgent.com publication.
© Copyright 2005 Hewlette & Levinson.

About the Author

Matt Jones, founder and CEO of FavoriteAgent.com, built a very successful real estate company in a hurry. His business sense and managerial capabilities came from twenty years in the transmission business. His innovativeness and determination, however, arose from a less conspicuous source: he was looking failure in the face, and he didn't like what he saw.

Only three years ago, having decided to change careers mid-stream, he went back to school, got a real estate license, and began to follow everybody's advice about what to do next. Trouble was, the traditional methods and formulas, and even all the many hours on the job, didn't work for him. By doing what everybody else was doing, he was getting mediocre results for the first time in his life. And he wasn't earning much of a living! So he re-invented the system.

With FavoriteAgent.com, he developed a user-friendly, Internet-based real estate model that brought in many, many more customers and handled them effectively. In fact, during his first year as a REALTOR®, Matt listed 114 homes – all at 8% or more – in a very unremarkable market. Since then, he's grown from a single-agent local practice to a local team of over forty agents and a national team with agents in more than five hundred markets in fifty states and Canada. In short, the growth of his company has been phenomenal.

Matt willingly admits that he's been the right man with the right skills at the right time. And, since it's frustrating for him to see other REALTORS® working harder than ever before, yet getting fewer results for their work, he wants to share the secret of his success. He knows he's been blessed and feels compelled to give back. That's why he wrote *LCM*, and that's why he's made it available to you.

Matt Jones lives in Fayetteville, North Carolina, his home of twenty-two years, with his wife Theresa and their four children, two of whom are with him at FavoriteAgent.com.

Order Form

To order additional copies, fill out this form and send it along with your check or money order to: Favorite Agent Publishing, 4155 Ferncreek Drive, Fayetteville, NC 28314.

Cost per copy $16.00 plus $4.00 P&H.

Ship _____ copies of *LCM: The Secret to Success in the New Age of Real Estate* to:

Name_____

Address:_____

City/State/Zip:_____

___ Check for signed copy

Please tell us how you found out about this book.

___ Friend   ___ Internet
___ Book Store   ___ Radio
___ Newspaper   ___ Magazine